WOMEN ON THE FRONTLINE

Victorious Through Prayer, Faith, Courage, and Power!

SONYA MICHELLE SNELL

Women of God on the Frontline – Victorious Through Prayer, Faith, Courage, Worship, and Power

Copyright © 2024 All rights reserved—Sonya Michelle Snell

No part of this book may be reproduced or transmitted in any form or by any means, graphic, electronic, or mechanical, including photocopying, recording, taping, or by an information storage retrieval system without the written permission of the publisher. The contents and cover of this book may not be reproduced in whole or in part in any form without the express written permission of the author or B.O.Y. Enterprises, Inc.

Please direct all copyright inquiries to:

B.O.Y. Publications, Inc.
c/o Author Copyrights
P.O. Box 262
Lowell, NC 28098
betonyourselfent.com

Paperback ISBN: 978-1-955605-66-3

Cover and Interior Design: B.O.Y. Enterprises, Inc.

Printed in the United States of America.

Dedication

I would like to dedicate this book to my precious family, husband Ben, and children Jermir, Shyia, Jordan, Ephraim, and first grandchild, most adorable granddaughter Jade Victoria. You all inspire me daily to be my best and do my best. Without your support, love, prayers, and laughter I would not be the woman I am today!

ACKNOWLEDGMENTS

In memory of my dear sweet grandma, Mrs. Mamie Estelle Mallard Washington. Here's to you grandma for always being my rock! I love you and miss you sorely!

Praise for WOMEN OF GOD ON THE FRONTLINE

Come, journey with me in this inspiring devotional that prepares you when God places you on the frontline. With insights about Esther, a woman whose proof God can use the less likely to do great exploits through, Sonya Michelle Snell fuels your heart, mind, and spirit with tactical tools to keep you strong and courageous.
As she goes through these five advanced tactical units, you're sure to learn the following presented from the words of the author:

As with Esther, knowing our value in the Kingdom of God is vital!

It's not about you but about what God has placed before you for His people!

She describes the importance of a heart being synched with God's in prayer because it makes a difference. Regarding faith, only when we apply scriptures appropriately, we exercise biblical faith. God, in turn, gives us the courage to leave the outcome in His hands because you can't manipulate the results in your favor. And the power and presence of God in your life establishes a bridge which captures your inabilities and grants you His ability to achieve the impossible through Him. Above all, worship the Lord with our whole heart, and passion for Christ.
You owe it to yourself to walk in victory despite your circumstances. So, seeking a book to empower you to represent a woman on the frontline and break every chain, look no further. Sonya's engaging book will dazzle your mind and encourage you profoundly.

Vernita "Neat" Simmons
Author/Publishing Consultant and Speaker of
Sacred Moments With God

Table of Contents

Introduction 9
Women of God on the Frontline.................................. 10
Valuable Lessons from Esther 12
PRAYER 17
Faith... 22
Courage... 29
Worship 34
Power... 41
Revealing 47
Victorious 49
Greatest Turnaround… 54
When I Think of His Goodness… 56
Go … Do the Thing 59
What I Leave with You… 63
From My Heart to Yours 65
Scripture Unit 65
BREAKING EVERY CHAIN... 69
Decree and Declare 71
Victorious Reflections 83
ENDNOTES... 89
Come Let Us Fellowship 90
Meet The Author 91

Introduction

To know me, is to know I have a heart for women, which drives my passion to empower and encourage! I give all praise to my Lord and Savior Jesus Christ for His strength, love for, and faithfulness to me! I am grateful to God for impregnating me with the Women of God on the Frontline vision and allowing its fruition to be experienced and birthed through anointed conferences and now this inspiring book. I am humbled to be used by Him and forever grateful.

Women of God on the Frontline will forever be a part of my ministry as it was given by God to ensure and share with all women far and near, big or small, various backgrounds, different stories, that we are OF God. I cannot wait to share with you what God has placed in me through Women of God on the Frontline Victorious through Prayer, Faith, Courage, Worship, and Power, Breaking Every Chain!

Women of God on the Frontline

We as Women of God face many challenges. However, we are more than conquerors; we are survivors.

"For if thou altogether holdest thy peace at this time, then shall there enlargement and deliverance arise to the Jews from another place; but thou and thy father's house shall be destroyed: and who knoweth whether thou art come to the kingdom for such a time as this?" - **Esther 4:14**

We as Women of God face many challenges. However, we are more than conquerors; we are survivors. We are Women of God on The Frontline Victorious through prayer, faith, courage, worship, and power, and breaking every chain!

As with Esther, knowing our value in the Kingdom of God is vital! There comes a time when we may need to perform roles other than the ones we have become accustomed to doing. Rest assured, as this occurs we will be given the Lord's grace to continue to represent Him while breaking every chain!

Valuable Lessons from Esther

Esther was an orphan. God still exalted her and used her. Your background does not decide what God can do in and through you.

Victorious Through Prayer, Faith, Courage, and Power!

We can gather many lessons from the study of the life of Esther. For now, we will examine four of these lessons: There is a time of preparation, the importance of the favor of God, God works in His own time and season, and recognizing your background does not hinder your future. Let's dive in

There Is a Time of Preparation

Esther sanctioned herself to be prepared for the task. As we experience God's preparation time, it may feel like the journey is long and uneventful. However, the refining of our character is essential to God's plan for our life. God cannot use a proud woman.

The Importance of the Favor of God

Esther obtained favor with the King. When you live a life pleasing to God, by obeying His will, you will gain favor with Him, resulting in favor with people as well.

God Works in His Own Time and Season

Esther got her timing right! Maybe God has placed a calling on your life. Don't leap into it without preparation. Instead, wait for God's timing and alignment. God will move in His time when we stay faithful and alert to His leading.

Our Background Does Not Hinder Our Future

Esther was an orphan. God still exalted her and used her. Your background does not decide what God can do in and through you. Your faith does! I am often reminded God is no respecter of persons. (Acts 10:34) He used and still uses women to accomplish His untiring ministry in a world of need. With God, your background will never hinder your future!

Now…take a journey with me as I expound on the words Women of God on the Frontline. In this section, I will describe why I take pride in knowing who I am and whose I am.

First - *Women of God*, the word **OF** is defined to indicate origin, from content or material. (1).

If we declare that we are women **OF** God, then we are declaring that we originate from Him, we have His attributes, contents … meaning we have all that we need within us to be victorious! Why? Because our Father is victorious in all things! Esther, a Woman of God, was given everything she needed to complete her kingdom task! Oh, and He will do the same for you!

Second - *Frontline* -is defined as the most forward position of an armed force, a military line formed by the most advanced tactical combat units, an area of potential or actual conflict or struggle, the most advanced responsible visible position in a field or activity. (2)

Women of God we are on the frontline, and it is time that we band together and form the most forward positioned spiritual line of prayer, faith, courage, worship, and power against the enemy. Our spiritual line must be unbreakable and unmovable; focused on building God's kingdom and the tearing down of Satan's.

Esther in chapter 4:16 sent answer back to Mordecai stating Go, gather together all the Jews that are present in Shushan, and fast you for me, and neither eat nor drink three days, night or day: I also and my maidens will fast likewise; and so, will I go in to the king, which is not according to the law: and if I perish, I perish.

She immediately took her place on the frontline for the people of God! I pray that by the time you have read this book in its entirety that you will remember it's not about you but about what God has placed before you for His people.

The First part of the Frontline definition: a military line formed by the most advanced tactical combat units.

Spiritual Advanced Tactical Units: Prayer and Faith

Tactical is defined as relating to or constituting actions carefully planned to gain a specific military end. (3)

Prayer and faith are part of the preparation process! It took prayer and faith for Esther, and it's going to take that for us women of God as well to move forward in victory! We will learn how to use prayer and faith on the frontline as it is designed by God.

PRAYER

Do you find it at all instructive that Jesus found it necessary to pray? If He did not feel He could face the battle in His own strength; neither should we.

True prayer is honest, humble and personal. It is a great privilege. Can you think of any greater honor than to have an audience with the One who rules over ALL creation? We have been invited to talk with the one who put the stars in place. We are invited to seek counsel from the One who is truth and wisdom. We are invited to sit down with the One who knows all things. Prayer is a privilege purchased by the blood of Jesus Christ. Having a conversation is a part of any vital and growing relationship. Often the quality of relationships is measured by the presence of communication. Or to state it another way, one of the first things people point to as evidence that a relationship is in trouble is a lack of communication. The same is true for our relationship with the Father.

True, honest, heartfelt conversation is a sign of a healthy relationship. A lack of conversation is a sign of a relationship in trouble. Constantly we are warned of the Devil's intention to neutralize and demoralize us. We are told that "our struggle is not against flesh and blood, but against the rulers, against the authorities, against the powers of this dark world and against the spiritual forces of evil in the heavenly realms." (Ephesians 6:10).

We are in a battle, and we need the help of God. The enemy has marshaled his armies so when we neglect prayer, we go into battle unarmed. Do you find it at all instructive that Jesus found it necessary to pray? If He did not feel He could face the battle in His own strength; neither should we. We should pray because we are in a fierce battle. Our battle is not a natural fight it is a spiritual fight. So, when we face our spiritual frontline battles do not try to win with natural weapons. Prayer is a shield that able us to stand firm against any distractions of sin in our lives. In the quiet times of private, honest prayer, God exposes the rationalizations and the excuses that we use to cater to sin. In prayer, God holds a mirror up to our lives so we can see the way we really are and repent.

Esther had to get herself together and after praying God stood up inside of her and revealed to her what she needed to do! Prayer makes a difference. Prayer is a way to talk to God for people. I know that circumstances change when we pray. Diseases are healed, strength is imparted, guidance is given, hearts are softened, needs are met. I know that when I pray for others, it helps them. But I also know that when I pray, I am changed.

Scripture Unit

> Do not be anxious about anything, but in everything by prayer and supplication with thanksgiving let your requests be made known to God. And the peace of God, which surpasses all understanding, will guard your hearts and your minds in Christ Jesus.
>
> -Philippians 4:6-7

Prayer Unit

Father God, I come to you in the Name of Jesus asking that you will empower me with a purpose driven, effective, and strong prayer life resulting in me becoming a better person drawn to you through prayer. I desire to seek you more each day while on the frontline. Help me, Father, to do just that. I receive and declare a victorious life on the Frontline through Prayer. Amen

Frontline Victorious Reflections:

Faith

As we can see from the example's faith is a response of our total being. It involves our mind in understanding and our spirit in perceiving spiritual reality. It also involves our will in choosing.

What is true faith?

True faith is essential for living a life pleasing to God. Biblical faith has two key elements. First, it is a belief in the truth. What we believe in must be based on facts, on what is true. Truth includes total reality, and total reality includes both the seen and the unseen realms. Belief in the truth in itself is, however, not true faith. There must be the second element: the appropriate response to the truth. In other words, we must be living out the truth.

Such a life, that is, the life of true faith, would mean trusting God and obeying Him, believing in His Word and living it out for He is the God of truth and His Word is the truth. It would mean living agreeing to what the Scriptures teach and according to God's guidance. It is a life based on an accurate understanding of the Scriptures - who God is and what He has truly revealed. If we misapply the Scriptures or are deceived, we won't be exercising biblical faith. The apostle Paul tells us this is the life of faith that God intends for all His children: "God has chosen you from the beginning for salvation through sanctification by the Spirit and faith in the truth" (2 Thessalonians 2:13). True faith results in a truly positive outcome.

In the many examples of faith cited, we see three aspects of true faith:

❖ First, knowing the truth.

- ❖ Second, living the truth.
- ❖ And third, the positive outcome.

The first two aspects are expressions of faith. The third shows us that ultimately, those who exercised true faith were not disappointed, for God rewarded them. Let's take a look at Noah in Hebrews 11:7. By faith Noah, being warned by God about things not yet seen, in reverence prepared an ark for the salvation of his household, by which he condemned the world, and became an heir of the righteousness which is according to faith.

Noah was warned by God about things not yet seen. Faith can involve things we have not yet seen or which we do not fully understand. Noah heard God, and he responded by preparing an ark. His obedient action led to the salvation of his household, and the pronouncement of the Scriptures that he was an heir of the righteousness according to faith. Noah was commended for his faith not merely because he acted on something difficult and which he did not fully understand. He was commended because he acted on God's instructions.

Esther was called. This was Esther appointment and once she realized God had anointed her life to save the Jews she walked in Faith. In my studying years ago, I heard God speak these words to me; "While being obedient, walk by faith."

Joshua walked around the Jericho wall having faith out of obedience to the voice of God! As we can see from the example's faith is a response of our total being. It involves our mind in understanding and our spirit in perceiving spiritual reality. It also involves our will in choosing. Unless we choose to respond appropriately to the truth we have come to understand, the response of faith is not yet complete.

Scripture Unit:

Proverbs 3:5-6 Trust in the LORD with all thine heart; and lean not unto thine own understanding. In all thy ways acknowledge him, and he shall direct thy paths.

-Proverbs 3:5-6

Prayer Unit:

Father God, I come to you in the Name of Jesus asking that you will empower me with the biblical faith you have imparted to me through your Word. Let me see your truth while on the Frontline and not the enemy distractions; that I may walk by faith and not by sight. I receive and declare a victorious life on The Frontline through Faith. Amen

Frontline Victorious Reflections:

The Second part of the Frontline definition: an area of potential or actual conflict or struggle. During this phase of being on the spiritual frontline, we must display courage and worship!

Courage

To be courageous, you must be aware that God is the one who is responsible for the outcome.

Biblical courage can merely originate from one source to be valid. Biblical courage is not the result of self-reliance or self-confidence. Biblical courage is the result of surrender and sovereignty. Our surrender to God's sovereignty, and our trust in God's strength, not on our own! There are, of course, many places in Scripture where you can witness courage. However, Joshua shines brightly. There you have all the ingredients of the impossible, but Joshua took courage! Joshua had experienced deep personal loss. He just lost his spiritual father. Moses was dead.

"Moses my servant is dead; now, therefore, arise, cross this Jordan, you and all this people, to the land which I am giving them, even to the children of Israel." Joshua has presented the only valid source of strength. "⁵No man will be able to stand before you all the days of your life: as I was with Moses, so I will be with you. I will not fail you or forsake you." So, the basis of Joshua's courage was to be the presence of God in his life, the promise of God in his heart, and the power of God on his behalf. With that in place, God gave Joshua an order! "⁶Be strong and courageous, for you shall give this people possession of the land which I swore to their fathers to give them."

Have not I commanded you? Be strong and courageous! Do not tremble or be dismayed, for the LORD your God is with you, wherever you go. -Joshua 1:2, 5-6, 9

For just a moment let us view the biblical definition of the word. It involves four facts.

1. To be courageous is an order. Therefore, it is a choice of the will. Remember, God only orders us to do what He empowers us to do.

2. To be courageous is a must. For God to be exalted and God's people to inherit the land, Joshua and his host had no choice. Either they trusted God, or they didn't. They couldn't change the odds or the enemy. All they could do was decide whether or not to be strong. Either they were courageous, or they missed the blessing.

3. To be courageous, you must be aware that God is the one who is responsible for the outcome. "Be not afraid, neither be thou dismayed" the King James phrase is, "for the LORD your God is with you whithersoever thou goest." I gave you the land, God reminded Joshua, so the battle isn't yours, it's MINE. No wonder you can be strong!

The results aren't up to you.

4- To be courageous is to consciously draw upon the quality of God's character from within you that lets you trust Him with the outcome and with your well-being, merely resting in His sovereignty. Biblical courage, then, is "supernatural confidence in the sovereignty of God in the face of danger or difficulty." It results in the awareness that God has become responsible for both the battle and the outcome!

God's power is not limited, and He is in total control. His benevolence is seen in Esther's courageous life. Without her fearlessness, her story would be different. The events in our lives are in God's hands. God who is so concerned for us is able to change our pain into joy.

Scripture Unit:

Be on your guard; stand firm in the faith; be courageous; be strong.

-1 Corinthians 16:13

Prayer Unit:

Father God, I come to you in the Name of Jesus asking that you will empower me to be courageous in and through you. Help me to not focus on the outcome or my ability in itself while on the frontline. But help me to stay laser focus on whose I am and to take courage knowing that I can do all things through Christ who strengthens me. I receive and declare a victorious life on the Frontline through Courage. Amen.

Frontline Victorious Reflections:

Worship

In spirit and in truth...

The purpose of our worship is to glorify, honor, praise, exalt, and please God. Our worship must show our adoration and loyalty to God for His grace in providing us with the way to escape the bondage of sin, so we can have the salvation He so much wants to give us.

James 4:6, 10 tells us, "God resists the proud, but gives grace to the humble. Humble yourselves in the sight of the Lord, and He will lift you up". Our worship to God is a very humble and devout action.

Jesus says in John 4:23-24, "But the hour is coming, and now is, when true worshippers will worship the Father in spirit and in truth, for the Father is seeking such to worship Him. God is a spirit and they that worship Him must worship Him in spirit and in truth." It doesn't say we can worship God any way we want, but we must worship Him in spirit and in truth. The word must make it absolute. There is no other way we can worship God and be acceptable to Him. The word "must", expresses "an obligation, a requirement, a necessity, a certainty, and something that must be done". (4)

When must is used it means it is not optional. Here the word "must" is expressing this is the only way to acceptably worship God. God is after true worshippers. And He identifies them as those who worship Him in spirit and in truth. Worshipping God with such honor is a deep matter which must not be taken lightly. If we have any regard for our own souls, we will want to make sure we are worshipping God in spirit and in truth. Worship is a time when we pay deep, sincere, awesome respect, love, and fear to the one who created us. Acts 17:24-25 says, "God who made the world and everything in it, since He is Lord of heaven and earth, does not dwell in temples made with hands, as though He needed anything since He gives life, breath, and all things." Worship should cause us to reflect on the majesty and graciousness of God, contrasted to our own unworthiness. God does not have to have our worship, but we must worship Him to please Him. Our singing, praying, studying His Word, giving, and communion are designed by God to bring us closer to Him and to cause us to think more like He thinks, thus becoming more like Him. James 4:8 tells us to, "Draw near to God and He will draw near to you."

Our worship not only honors and magnifies God, but it is also for our own edification and strength. Worship helps us develop a Christ-like character. We become like unto those we admire and worship. When we worship God, we tend to value what God values and gradually take on the characteristics and qualities of God, but never to His level. As Philippians 2:5 says, "Let this mind be in you which was also in Christ." How do we take on the mind of Christ? In Romans 12:2 we read, "And do not be conformed to this world, but be transformed by the renewing of your mind." We renew our mind as we study and meditate on God's Word and worship Him. When we worship God, we develop such traits as forgiveness, tenderness, justice, righteousness, purity, kindness, and love. All of this is preparing us for eternal life in heaven with God. As we are told in Colossians 3:2 to, "Set your mind on things above, and not on things on the earth."

Scripture Unit

> But the hour cometh, and now is, when the true worshippers shall worship the Father in spirit and in truth: for the Father seeketh such to worship him.
>
> -John 4:23

Prayer Unit

Father God, I come to you in the Name of Jesus asking that you will empower me with the right mind of worship. That I may come before you and bow in spirit and in truth to worship you for who you are and not merely for what you can do for me. Let me be pleasing to you, Father God through my worship while on the frontline. I declare and receive a victorious life on the Frontline through Worship. Amen.

Frontline Victorious Reflections:

Third part of Frontline definition: responsible or visible position in a field or activity. When on the frontline the enemy should be able to witness the power of God in your life!

Victorious Through Prayer, Faith, Courage, and Power!

Power

In the gospel, God confronts us with our utter inability to accomplish anything of value apart from Him… "The Power of God in our lives.

The dangerous assumption we unknowingly accept in the American dream is that our greatest asset is our own ability. The gospel beckons us to die to ourselves and to believe in God and to trust in His power. In the gospel, God confronts us with our utter inability to accomplish anything of value apart from Him…The Power of God in our Lives.

In First Chronicles 13:14, David, the great king of Israel wanted to go and retrieve the Ark of the Covenant which represented the very presence and power of God.
1 Chronicles 13:5 says, *"So David gathered all Israel together, from Shihor in Egypt to as far as the entrance of Hamath, to bring the ark of God from Kirjath Jearim."* On the way back one of the Israelite men, Uzzah, touched the Ark and died. So instead of taking the Ark into the City of David, the King decided to take the Ark to the house of a man called Obed-Edom.

"The ark of God remained with the family of Obed-Edom in his house three months. And the Lord blessed the house of Obed-Edom and all that he had." -1 Chronicles 13:14

QUESTION: What was so special about the Ark that when it was left at the home of Obed-Edom, that his entire house received a blessing?

The answer is the Ark contained the very Presence and Power of God. The Presence and Power of God changed Obed-Edom's home. The Bible declares that his house and ALL that was in it was blessed. This blessing was in response to the presence and power of God moving into his life. When we allow God to come in and start blessing us, He will transform our lives. Without the power and presence of God in our lives, we will be living under our own power.

God is our father, and yes, we are His children, however, we are children with power. Whether we chose to use it or not is up to us, but either way, we have it. The Holy Spirit has given you power so that whatever place you find yourself on the frontline, you need to know you have the power that is necessary to sustain you into that place in which you are called.

How many of us are happy to live our lives without the power of God?

How many of us are willing to attend a church without the evidence of the power of God?

How many of us speak about worship, but never experience the power of God?

God makes available to us through His power

1. To know and believe the Truth.

2. To become a Child of God.

3. To Resist Every Temptation.

4. To Endure Suffering and Hardship.

5. To Serve Others.

What methods does God use to provide this Power? This power does us no good unless we know how to obtain it.

- ❖ There Is Power in Jesus' Blood.
- ❖ There Is Power in God's Love.
- ❖ There Is Power in the Scriptures.
- ❖ There Is Power in Prayer.
- ❖ There Is Power in associating with other Christians.

Scripture Unit

"And what [is] the exceeding greatness of his power to us-ward who believe, according to the working of his mighty power." **-Ephesians 1:19**

Prayer Unit

Father God, I come to you in the Name of Jesus asking that you will empower me with your power that I may able to see your glory while on the frontline. Endow me with your power that's able to move mountains, heal the sick, raise the dead, and love as only you can. I receive and declare a victorious life on the Frontline through Power. Amen.

Frontline Victorious Reflections:

_____
_____
_____
_____
_____
_____
_____
_____
_____
_____
_____
_____
_____
_____
_____
_____
_____
_____
_____
_____

Prayer, Faith, Courage, Worship, Power of God,
…can break every chain!

Revealing

God's Sovereignty - The hand of God is at work in the lives of His people. He used the circumstances in Esther's life, as He uses the decisions and actions of all humans to providentially work out His divine plans and purposes. We can trust in the Lord's sovereign care over every aspect of our lives.

God's Deliverance - The Lord raised up Esther, as He raised up Moses, Joshua, Joseph, and many others to deliver His people from destruction. Through Jesus Christ, we are delivered from death and hell. God is able to save His children.

Frontline Victorious Reflections:

Victorious

Esther had gone up in the world and had achieved a position of power and distinction, it required strength and beauty of character for her still to love and remember the so-called simple people from whom she sprang.

Are you feeling victorious yet? I sure hope so! Because you are through Christ! No matter what it feels like, look like, in fact, no matter what it really and truly is right now you are still victorious because our Father causes you to be!! Because of HIM, we ARE! Don't allow your circumstances to rob you. You have to be bigger than what you are facing right now. Feelings can hinder us from exercising our faith in God! Remember faith moves on trusting that when the first step is taken the next will be revealed! I hear chains falling in your lives right now! Break Chains… Break!

Our Father is a good Father! He cares about each one of us. I am victorious, you are victorious. In my Oprah's voice "You get to be Victorious, and you get to be victorious, and you get to be victorious, and you get to be victorious"!!! We all get to be victorious! In the Name of Jesus! Do you believe it? Do not allow the enemy to stop you from exercising your right to walk in victory.

I decree that God is going to give you double for your trouble. I've always heard that said. "Double for your trouble" but didn't realize it's indeed biblical. It is in the Word, Sisters. For every trouble you go through on the frontline God will give you double the blessing. (Zachariah 9:12). Those that hope in Christ tirelessly can expect double.

We're accustomed to counting our abundant blessings, but I say to you to count your troubles because, for every frontline experience, God is going to restore you twice as much! Are you qualified for the double? You get a BOGO; you get a 2 for 1. Double for you trouble. Be encouraged you are victorious even in your troubles because double shall be yours. Restoration is here.

Take Part....

We all know the story of Esther. If you aren't familiar, I encourage you to read all about how God brought Esther to the throne for such a time as this. How Esther went from her exile and poverty to be the queen of the greatest empire in those times on the face of the earth. Although God is never mentioned in the book not once His presence, providing, and power is felt throughout this incredible book. So are the days of our lives. At times, God may seem as if He is hiding, but Women of God on The Frontline be encouraged, seen or unseen He always completes that which is according to His will.

Esther, that extraordinary woman of God on the frontline, was a mixture of strength, charisma, and skill; she was a woman of God on the frontline whose character was secure

from the root of power, prosperity, and power. Esther had gone up in the world and had achieved a position of power and distinction, it required strength and beauty of character for her still to love and remember the so-called simple people from whom she sprang. Lord help us to remember you cannot use a proud woman.

Witnessing to the rock from which she came, Esther dared to risk death for her people and so escaped dying with them. You may be tempted to say; If only I was Esther with countless opportunities what I wouldn't do to glorify God. Realize that all around you are opportunities of serving God and a needy world. We are women of God on the frontline victorious through prayer, faith, courage, worship, and power breaking every chain.

Victorious Through Prayer, Faith, Courage, and Power!

God invites us to join His work, not for His sake, but for ours.

God invited Esther to join Him in saving the Jewish nation. If Esther had refused to go to the King, God still would have saved His people, but she would have missed an opportunity. Have you ever experienced missed opportunities to be a blessing to someone, to pray for someone, to encourage someone, to better yourself, etc.? Our refusal to take part in God's work does not hinder God. It limits our privilege to take part in what He is doing. God's foresight is comprehensive, wise, and holy. His timing and calling are no mistake, and He has placed us Women of God On The Frontline as Esther, here, now, and for such a time as this.

Greatest Turnaround…

We do not always get to see the who, what, when, where's or loose ends, but that does not mean things are not coming together.

As Esther allowed herself to be used, God was planning the most remarkable turnaround. Oh yes!! What meant for bad Jesus will turn it around for your good! God's hand of divine intervention was moving to set things right, to tie up the loose ends before the story even began.

We can witness it working out by looking at the turnarounds.

1. When Vashti is called, she refuses to come, however, Esther is not called but shows up.
2. The Kings honor goes to Mordecai instead of Haman.
3. Haman is condemned at the feast when he expects to be honored.
4. The gallows intended for Mordecai are used for Haman.

All these turnarounds point us to the greatest U-turn of all: Christ came to undo the fall. He took Adam's disaster, our disasters, and in a most unforeseen way, He conquered death and gave us life. (Romans 5:17).

Have you had any situations where you thought all hope was lost only to encounter the very hand of God that would come in and turn things around just like that! When you just knew it was our good Father that was all up and in it! Have you ever wondered how it will all work out?

We do not always get to see the who, what, when, where's or loose ends, but that does not mean things are not coming together. God is at work!! Remember while being obedient to God walk by Faith.

When I Think of His Goodness…

Remembering God's faithfulness in the past gives us the courage to believe in His faithfulness for the future.

Memories are powerful. Habitually and deliberately recalling the goodness of our God is an act of faithfulness, which reconditions the fullness and joy of our salvation. Remembering our past also gives us a new perspective through which to view the future. How have you seen God's faithfulness in your life? Remembering God's faithfulness in the past gives us the courage to believe in His faithfulness for the future, women of God on the frontline.

From Esther character, we learn:
1. To seek divine guidance in times of difficulty (4:15-17).
2. To obtain a knowledge of human nature, so that we may know how to take advantage of any circumstances which may favor our cause.
3. When there is a necessity, to be ready to renounce self and exert ourselves for the good of others.
4. To value and seek the cooperation of fellow-believers.

Dealing with the ultimate safety of the Jews, which Esther secured, we learn:
1. To have unbounded confidence in God's providence, and not to undervalue small things.
2. To acknowledge God as the Author of all mercies.

Frontline Victorious Reflections

Go ... Do the Thing

I say to you Sister, go do the thing! It's yours, and you can do it. I encourage you to accept and celebrate your calling.

Esther's calling was about seeing her life from the perspective of how God saw her, and the story God was crafting for her life. As with you, you have a calling. I invite you to see yourself through the eyes of your heavenly Father. He made you and knows all about you. He has declared a life for you that eyes haven't seen, and ears haven't heard. See yourself as the daughter of the King, and reach for your calling. Every single one of us has a calling, an assignment. And just like Esther, the day is coming when we are going to have to give an account to our Father on how we used our gifts, talents, and time that He entrusted to us. He will not ask you about Esther or your next sister's assignment, but he is going to ask about yours. What have you been doing? Where have you been spending your time? Have you executed the assignments I've prepared you for?

Once Esther connected with her assignment she executed with no other agenda, no other priority but that of the assignment that was placed in her hand to do. She didn't look for the applause of man or the easy way out to remain safe and secure in her position in the background. No, the courage, authority, and power of God stood up in her, and she carried out the task at hand to help save her people. I'm encouraging you to get busy living in the calling God has called you for. We all have a ministry. Ministry to serve, love, nurture, give, smile, share our talents and gifts. Do not be afraid to walk in the calling that God has for your life. I say to you Sister, go do the thing! It's yours, and you can do it. I encourage you to accept and celebrate your calling.

God graciously gave Esther the power and authority she needed. She did not have to be afraid that she was not equipped for her calling. It was her calling. Esther did not walk in shoes that weren't hers. She stayed in her lane. If you walk in what God has for you, you will have more than enough to sustain you because it's yours. God does not call you because you are already equipped. He calls you, and for those who will say yes, He will equip you with exactly what you need to sustain you in that calling. Oh, the enemy hopes that you will go in your own power. Women of God on the Frontline, rest in God's power. God's power will make you that great wife, mother, entrepreneur, that women ministry. Trust in God.

God sent Esther. God does the sending. Let God do the sending. Resist the urge to send yourself to do an assignment you have unprepared to do, or is not the time for. Just as important is your calling, so is the timing it is to work out in your life. Esther got her timing right. Had Esther moved, or not move in God's timing she would have truly perished. So, wait until God says go! I declare to you that waiting on God is the exact thing to do. Lord help us to wait for your time and season. If you give birth too early

to an assignment, you will abort the character Jesus is trying to birth in you. Had Esther moved too soon, neglecting the necessary training she endured during her preparation to become Queen Ester, she most likely would have made a mess of things because her character did not go through the necessary preparation of God's timing.

Esther's character required strength, beauty, and humility of character to love and remember her people from which she came while she sat in a powerful position in which she had achieved. Don't forsake the preparation process before going. It is vital to the building of your character.

Go, do the thing! Everything your calling requires is in your hand. Whatever you need, you got it. It is inside of you. Pull it out. Just as with Esther, it is within you, it's in there. Tap into it. God's favor is upon you. God's favor can open doors no man can shut! God's favor can position you for greatness. Women of God on the Frontline you are victorious! Victorious through God. Go do the thing.

What I Leave with You...

We're to grow in the faith which is our reaction to His truth.

Be courageous knowing God is in control of the outcome.

Women of God let's not back down from the enemy. If God has placed something, someone, someplace on your heart that's in need of your prayer, faith, courage, worship, and God's power move forward in breaking every chain! Let's strengthen our prayer life which is our relationship with God. We're to grow in the faith which is our reaction to His truth. Be courageous knowing God is in control of the outcome. And worship Him for who He is, knowing that everything around you may change day-to-day, but our God never changes and neither should our worship. And last, but not least declare the never-failing power of God which is His anointing and presence in your life that will ultimately break every chain!!

From My Heart to Yours Scripture Unit

I had fainted, unless I had believed to see the goodness of the Lord in the land of the living.

-Psalms 27:13

Psalm 27 1-14: ¹The LORD *is* my light and my salvation; whom shall I fear? the LORD *is* the strength of my life; of whom shall I be afraid?

²When the wicked, *even* mine enemies and my foes, came upon me to eat up my flesh, they stumbled and fell.

³Though an host should encamp against me, my heart shall not fear: though war should rise against me, in this *will* I *be* confident.

⁴One *thing* have I desired of the LORD, that will I seek after; that I may dwell in the house of the LORD all the days of my life, to behold the beauty of the LORD, and to inquire in his temple.

⁵For in the time of trouble he shall hide me in his pavilion: in the secret of his tabernacle shall he hide me; he shall set me up upon a rock.

⁶And now shall mine head be lifted up above mine enemies round about me: therefore, will I offer in his tabernacle sacrifices of joy; I will sing, yea, I will sing praises unto the LORD.

⁷Hear, O LORD, *when* I cry with my voice: have mercy also upon me, and answer me.

⁸When thou saidst, Seek ye my face; my heart said unto thee, Thy face, LORD, will I seek.

Victorious Through Prayer, Faith, Courage, and Power!

⁹Hide not thy face *far* from me; put not thy servant away in anger: thou hast been my help; leave me not, neither forsake me, O God of my salvation.

¹⁰When my father and my mother forsake me, then the LORD will take me up.

¹¹Teach me thy way, O LORD, and lead me in a plain path, because of mine enemies.

¹²Deliver me not over unto the will of mine enemies: for false witnesses are risen up against me, and such as breathe out cruelty.

¹³*I had fainted,* unless I had believed to see the goodness of the LORD in the land of the living.

¹⁴Wait on the LORD: be of good courage, and he shall strengthen thine heart: wait, I say, on the LORD.

From My Heart to Yours Prayer Unit

Father God, in the name of Jesus I come to you on behalf of my sister. I celebrate knowing that she is a new creature and now see herself in ways she's never seen before with all things becoming new. Order her steps, Lord. Allow her to trust you with her destiny, Lord. Thank you, Father for taking on all of her weakness, her mistakes, her limitations putting them on the cross and to death. Just as you were raised free and victorious because she is in you and of you, she has no limits. Holy Spirit, fill her up, order her steps, give her power and clarity to walk in the path that destiny has ordained. I thank you for new beginnings, fear is gone, and distractions be gone. I decree today that my sister is free in the Name of Jesus from everything that would hold her back. Yokes are broken, strongholds are broken. Nothing will have dominion over her life. Jesus, she is yours. I thank you for seeing her, now lead her. In Jesus Name!

Love you much,

Sonya Michelle Snell

BREAKING EVERY CHAIN

Remember to be very selective with your battles. Sometimes peace is more honorable than always being right!

It matters what and who you take with you while on the frontline. Jesus makes the difference. If you are taking hurt, anger, frustration, defeat, excuses, etc. you are defeated already. Become that Woman of God on the Frontline victorious taking with you, prayer, faith, worship, courage, and power breaking every chain! Remember to be very selective with your battles. Sometimes peace is more honorable than always being right!

Decree and Declare

I confess, I proclaim, I declare, I believe,

therefore, *have I spoken.*

I repossess the land that I have lost, in the name of Jesus. I repossess supernatural financing to rebuild every broken place. I repossess and inhabit every possession stolen from me. I repossess my job, my health, my business, my marriage in Jesus name. I repossess my financial break-throughs. I retrieve my blessings in the name of Jesus, I repossess my victory. I confess I am delivered from the power of darkness. My battles belong to the Lord; He will fight all my battles, and I will triumph over my enemies in the name of Jesus. I repossess my vision. I confess that abundance of new ideas and favors are mine in the name of Jesus. I decree that I AM A Woman Of God On The Frontline Victorious Through Prayer, Faith, Worship, Courage, and Power, And Breaking Every Chain!

I confess, I proclaim, I declare, I believe, therefore, have I spoken.

Tacticals to Build, Strengthen, and Renew

I encourage you to use the scriptures listed at the end of the book as tactics to help build, strengthen and renew you as you embrace being a Woman of God on the Frontline Victorious!

I ask that you study one verse every day for a month to strengthen your prayer life. Chose the verses that minister to you the most and write them down to memorize and renew you. My prayer is that you will share this book with someone who needs encouragement to keep pressing when they see and feel the pressure of being on the frontline.

PRAYER

"Therefore, I tell you, whatever you ask in prayer, believe that you have received it, and it will be yours." -**Mark 11:24**

"Rejoice always. Pray without ceasing, give thanks in all circumstances; for this is the will of God in Christ Jesus for you. Do not quench the Spirit." -**1 Thessalonians 5:16-19**

"Do not be anxious about anything, but in everything by prayer and supplication with thanksgiving let your requests be made known to God. And the peace of God, which surpasses all understanding, will guard your hearts and your minds in Christ Jesus." -**Philippians 4:6-7**

"Therefore, confess your sins to one another and pray for one another, that you may be healed. The prayer of a righteous person has great power as it is working." -**James 5:16**

"And this is the confidence that we have toward him, that if we ask anything according to his will he hears us. And if we know that he hears us in whatever we ask, we know that we have the requests that we have asked." **-1 John 5:14-15**

"If any of you lacks wisdom, let him ask God, who gives generously to all without reproach, and it will be given him."
-**James 1:5**

FAITH

"Therefore, I say unto you, What things so ever ye desire, when ye pray, believe that ye receive them, and ye shall have them." **- Mark 11:24**

"That he would grant you, according to the riches of his glory, to be strengthened with might by his Spirit in the inner man; That Christ may dwell in your hearts by faith; that ye, being rooted and grounded in love." **-Ephesians 3:16-17**

"Now faith is the substance of things hoped for, the evidence of things not seen." **-Hebrews 11:1**

"But let him ask in faith, nothing wavering. For he that wavereth is like a wave of the sea driven with the wind and tossed." **-James 1:6**

"But without faith it is impossible to please him: for he that cometh to God must believe that he is and that he is a rewarder of them that diligently seek him." **-Hebrews 11:6**

"Jesus saith unto her, Said I not unto thee, that, if thou wouldest believe, thou shouldest see the glory of God?" **-John 11:40**

COURAGE

And the Lord, he it is that doth go before thee; he will be with thee, he will not fail thee, neither forsake thee: fear not, neither be dismayed.

-Deuteronomy 31:8

Have not I commanded thee? Be strong and of a good courage; be not afraid, neither be thou dismayed: for the Lord thy God is with thee whithersoever thou goest.

-Joshua 1:9

Blessed be God, even the Father of our Lord Jesus Christ, the Father of mercies, and the God of all comfort; Who comforteth us in all our tribulation, that we may be able to comfort them which are in any trouble, by the comfort wherewith we ourselves are comforted of God.

-2 Corinthians 1:3-4

Yea, though I walk through the valley of the shadow of death, I will fear no evil: for thou art with me; thy rod and thy staff they comfort me.

-Psalm 23:4

Be strong and of a good courage, fear not, nor be afraid of them: for the Lord thy God, he it is that doth go with thee; he will not fail thee, nor forsake thee.

–Deuteronomy 31:6

Wait on the Lord: be of good courage, and he shall strengthen thine heart: wait, I say, on the Lord. -Psalms 27:14

WORSHIP

O Lord, thou art my God; I will exalt thee, I will praise thy name; for thou hast done wonderful things; thy counsels of old are faithfulness and truth.

-Isaiah 25:1 -reliability God

Let every thing that hath breath praise the Lord. Praise ye the Lord.

-Psalm 150:6

And at midnight Paul and Silas prayed, and sang praises unto God: and the prisoners heard them.

-Acts 16:25 -prayer listening

God is a Spirit: and they that worship him must worship him in spirit and in truth.

-John 4:24 -truth Spirit

Bless the Lord, O my soul: and all that is within me, bless his holy name.

-Psalm 103:1 -holiness soul

O give thanks unto the Lord; for he is good; for his mercy endureth for ever.

-1 Chronicles 16:34 -gratitude

O God, thou art my God; early will I seek thee: my soul thirsteth for thee, my flesh longeth for thee in a dry and thirsty land, where no water is. Let my mouth be filled with thy praise and with thy honour all the day.

-Psalm 63:1

Thine, O Lord is the greatness, and the power, and the glory, and the victory, and the majesty: for all that is in the heaven and in the earth is thine; thine is the kingdom, O Lord, and thou art exalted as head above all.

-1 Chronicles 29:11 -kingdom strength almighty

POWER OF GOD

For the word of God is quick, and powerful, and sharper than any twoedged sword, piercing even to the dividing asunder of soul and spirit, and of the joints and marrow, and is a discerner of the thoughts and intents of the heart.

-Hebrews 4:12

Thine, O Lord is the greatness, and the power, and the glory, and the victory, and the majesty: for all that is in the heaven and in the earth is thine; thine is the kingdom, O Lord, and thou art exalted as head above all.

-1 Chronicles 29:11

Now unto him, that is able to do exceeding abundantly above all that we ask or think, according to the power that worketh in us, Unto him be glory in the church by Christ Jesus throughout all ages, world without end. Amen.

-Ephesians 3:20-21

The Lord is my strength and my shield; my heart trusted in him, and I am helped: therefore, my heart greatly rejoiceth; and with my song will I praise him.

-Psalm 28:7

VICTORIOUS... BREAKING EVERY CHAIN

For the LORD your God [is] he that goeth with you, to fight for you against your enemies, to save you.

-Deuteronomy 20:4

Isaiah 55:11 - So shall my word be that goeth forth out of my mouth: it shall not return unto me void, but it shall accomplish that which I please, and it shall prosper [in the thing] whereto I sent it.

-Isaiah 55:11

John 16:33 - These things I have spoken unto you, that in me ye might have peace. In the world ye shall have tribulation: but be of good cheer; I have overcome the world.

-John 16:33

For sin shall not have dominion over you: for ye are not under the law but under grace.

-Romans 6:14

[There is] therefore now no condemnation to them which are in Christ Jesus, who walk not after the flesh, but after the Spirit.
-Romans 8:1

What shall we then say to these things? If God [be] for us, who [can be] against us?

-Romans 8:31

Nay, in all these things we are more than conquerors through him that loved us.

-Romans 8:37

Victorious Reflections

Victorious Reflections

Victorious Through Prayer, Faith, Courage, and Power!

Victorious Reflections

Women of God on the Frontline

Victorious Reflections

Victorious Through Prayer, Faith, Courage, and Power!

Victorious Reflections

Women of God on the Frontline

Victorious Reflections

ENDNOTES

- Resources: All Scripture is taken from https://www.biblegateway.com/
- #1-4- **https://www.merriam-webster.com/**
- Images: **https://pixabay.com/en/**

Come Let Us Fellowship

Sonya Snell has a passion for women and is available to conduct workshops, conferences, and speaking engagements. Please contact and or follow her Here at her Facebook Page: https://www.facebook.com/WOGOTFL/

Meet The Author

A native of Holly Hill, SC; married to the love of her life Ben Snell and together we have four amazing children; Jermiroquan, DeAhjane, Jordan, and Jahnarious and one precious granddaughter; Jade Victoria. The daughter of Victoria Moorer and the late William Moorer.

Lady Sonya's has a heart for women; which drives her passion to empower and encourage. As a result, she was led by God to birth Women of God on the Frontline Ministries where she is the founder. This divine calling has also stirred her to host the Women of God the Frontline conferences for the past three years.

Encouraging all who attend to be spiritual sisters filled with purpose, power, strength, and faith-driven to make an impact on our families, communities, nations, and our legacies.

Her favorite scripture is Psalm 138:8 "The LORD will perfect that which concerneth me: thy mercy, O LORD, endureth forever: forsake not the works of thine own hands". Her favorite Bible character is Esther, and favorite song – My Redeemer Lives.

Milton Keynes UK
Ingram Content Group UK Ltd.
UKHW052100050724
444874UK00008B/53